Who Is Stevie Wonder?

by Jim Gigliotti

illustrated by Stephen Marchesi

Penguin Workshop

For Wendy, "My Cherie Amour"—JG

PENGUIN WORKSHOP
An Imprint of Penguin Random House LLC, New York

Published by Penguin Workshop, an imprint of Penguin Random House LLC, New York.
PENGUIN and PENGUIN WORKSHOP are trademarks of Penguin Books Ltd.
WHO HQ & Design is a registered trademark of Penguin Random House LLC.
Printed in the USA.

Visit us online at www.penguinrandomhouse.com.

Library of Congress Control Number: 2016033295

ISBN 9780448488585 10 9 8

Contents

Who Is Stevie Wonder?

Steveland Judkins walked into the Motown Record Corporation in Detroit, Michigan, one day in the fall of 1961. He was there to audition for the studio bosses. Every day, other musicians came to Motown for the same reason. They all hoped to become stars. Stevie, as he was called, was just like them—except that he was only eleven years old, and he was blind.

Stevie started off by playing the piano. Then he banged on the drums for a while. He was wearing dark sunglasses indoors, but plenty of young musicians thought wearing shades like that looked cool. And Stevie found his way around the instruments with no problem. Not everyone in the room realized Stevie was blind.

At first, Berry Gordy, who was the man in charge of Motown, didn't think Stevie was such a big deal. Gordy already had enough people who could play the piano and the drums. But after playing the drums, Stevie sang for a bit. Then he played the harmonica. Gordy was impressed that not only could Stevie do so many things well, but he did them with a wide smile on his face. Stevie clearly was enjoying himself, and everyone watching him was having a good time, too. Gordy decided then and there that he was going to sign Stevie to a recording contract.

That was more than fifty years ago. Today, Stevie is known around the world by his stage name, Stevie Wonder. He is a groundbreaking musician who has entertained millions of fans, performed in front of world leaders, and worked hard for social change. He has earned the highest honors awarded to composers, singers, musicians, and citizens of the United States. And he has done it all with the same positive attitude and wide smile on his face that he had in the Motown studio that day in 1961.

CHAPTER 1
Difficult Beginnings

Music had always been a big part of Stevie Wonder's life. He was still a baby when he began pounding on bongo drums in his crib. When he was a little boy, he grabbed whatever spoons he could find in the kitchen and played on the pots and pans. When he was about five years old, a barber on his street gave him a harmonica, and Stevie learned to play it. Stevie never had any formal lessons, but he always seemed to know how to make music with any instrument that was available.

Stevie was born as Steveland Hardaway Judkins on May 13, 1950, in Saginaw, Michigan. His mother's name was Lula Hardaway, and his father's name was Calvin Judkins. Stevie had two older brothers, Milton and Calvin Jr.

Two more brothers, Larry and Timmy, and a sister, Renee, were born in later years.

Stevie was born about six weeks earlier than expected. He probably was not blind when he was born. But when babies are born too early, they usually remain in the hospital until they are strong enough to go home. The hospital puts them in an incubator, which is supposed to keep conditions just right for them to be healthy. Stevie was in an incubator for more than a month.

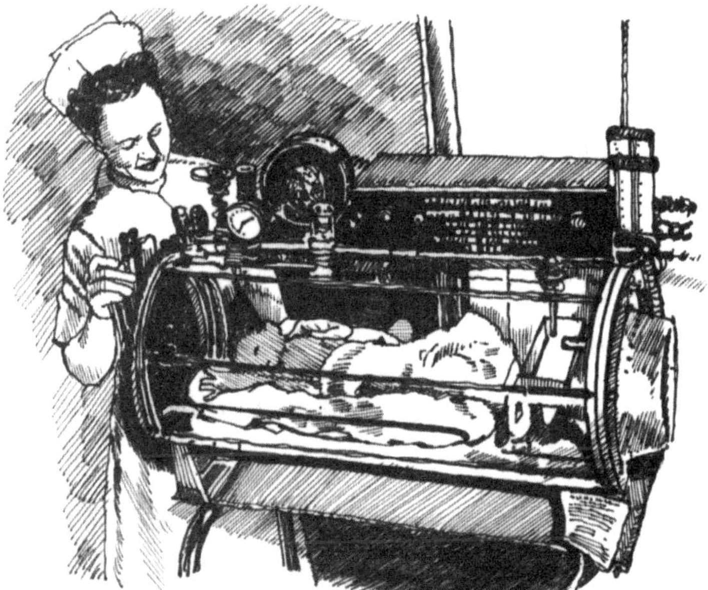

He seemed healthy in every way, except that doctors noticed his eyes didn't seem to respond to movement or light. They had not developed properly.

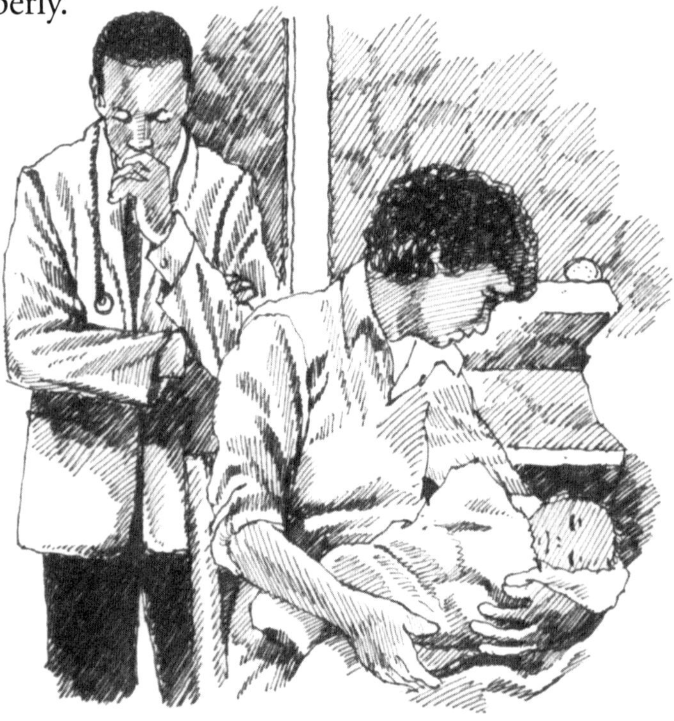

Naturally, Lula was upset at the news. She begged the doctors to do something to restore Stevie's sight, but there was nothing they could do. He was permanently blind.

Stevie couldn't see, but his hearing was incredible. When he was growing up, his siblings would drop a coin on a table. "What is it, Stevie?" they would ask. "A dime," Stevie would reply, correctly. They would drop another coin.

"How about that one?" they would ask. "A quarter," Stevie would say. Right again. Stevie's hearing was so good that he could identify the coin simply by the sound it made.

Stevie was so tuned in to sounds that naturally he was drawn to music. It started with the bongo drums in his crib. Stevie's father gave those to him. Calvin Sr. had been a pretty good musician himself, and he taught Stevie songs and encouraged his son's love for music. However, Calvin didn't have a regular job. He would sometimes leave the family for long periods of time. No one knew where he was or what he was doing. When Calvin was around, he wasn't very nice to Stevie's mother.

Lula thought that maybe in a bigger city Calvin could find a job and things would be better. So, when Stevie was four years old, the family moved about one hundred miles away to Detroit, on the eastern edge of Michigan.

Calvin joined Lula and the kids in Detroit, but he didn't change there. He still didn't work at a regular job, and he still went away sometimes.

Lula found a good job, though. Every morning, she would get up before the sun rose to work at a fish market. It was hard work, but she had a plan.

At the time, the family lived in an apartment that wasn't in a nice part of town. Lula wanted a better life for her kids. So she saved a little bit out of each paycheck and stuffed it under a mattress to hide it from Calvin.

When she had enough money, she made the first payment on a house in a good neighborhood. She moved there with her children, leaving Calvin behind.

CHAPTER 2
A Gift for Music

When Stevie was six years old, people in the Detroit area got to listen to a new radio station. On Sunday nights, the station played only the blues—a type of folk music created by black people in the southern part of the United States in the early 1900s.

Lula often had the radio on when she was home. She liked the blues. Every week Stevie was sure to tune in. By listening to the radio, Stevie became a big fan of musicians such as B. B. King, who became known as the "King of the Blues."

Even though Stevie was blind, his siblings never considered him handicapped.

Stevie went to a special school, the Fitzgerald Elementary School, but otherwise did most of the same things that his brothers did. "Some things he did better," Stevie's older brother Milton said.

B. B. King

Stevie liked to run around, climb trees, and even ride bikes. He would pedal while one of his brothers handled the steering.

Lula taught him not to feel sorry for himself because of his blindness, and she decided early

on that she wasn't going to be overprotective of him. Lula did, however, hold out hope that Stevie might one day see. She took him to different doctors. She even tried faith healers—preachers who believed that God could perform a miracle through them. They laid their hands on Stevie and prayed that God would let him see. But none of it worked.

Lula worried that Stevie would be unhappy because he was blind. But Stevie was happy. Finally, he told Lula one day, "Mama, you know maybe God doesn't mean for me to see. Maybe God meant for me to do something else."

It was apparent that "something else" was certainly going to include music.

Lula bought Stevie a cardboard drum set, and he quickly wore it out. A neighbor had a piano in her home and was delighted when Stevie came by to play. "Come over anytime," she told Stevie—and he did. When the woman moved away, she gave the piano to Stevie.

Stevie was eight years old when he went with Lula and his brothers to an outdoor concert at a neighborhood park. He caught the attention of the leader of the band. Stevie told him he was a musician, too. So the bandleader led him onto the stage and sat him down at the drums. Stevie wowed the crowd with his playing, and the bandleader gave him seventy-five cents. Stevie loved that he got paid to do something he really enjoyed!

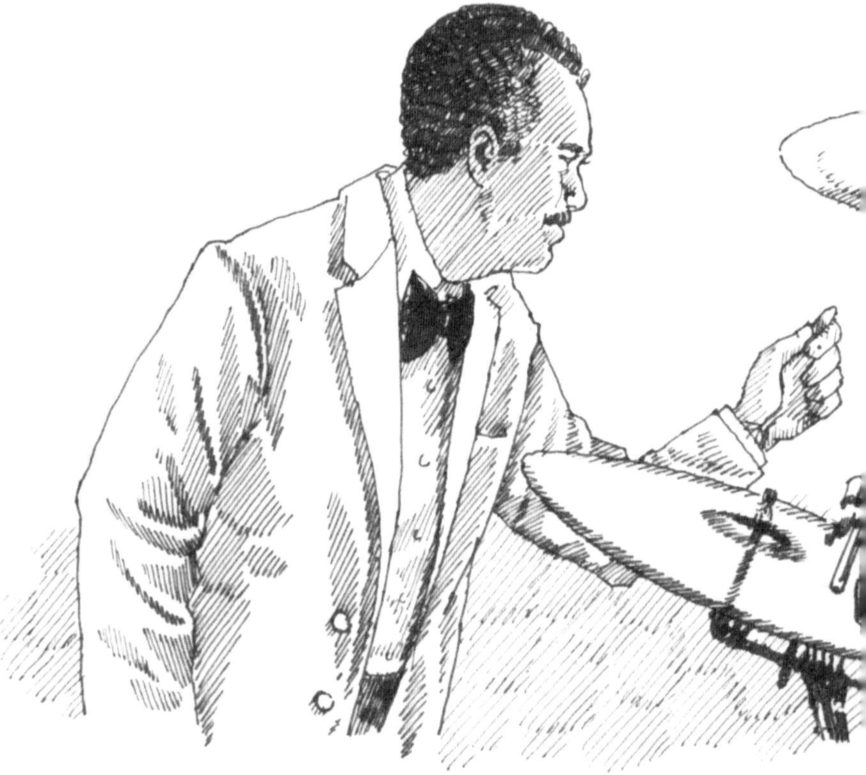

Stevie sang in the choir at Whitestone Baptist Church. Churchgoers loved to hear him sing gospel music at Sunday services. But one of the church leaders heard him singing rhythm-and-blues music in the neighborhood one day. Rhythm and blues, which was still rclatively new in the late 1950s, was not considered appropriate music by traditional churches. So Stevie was asked to leave his church choir.

R&B

Rhythm and blues (called R&B for short) is a style of music that combines parts of gospel, jazz, country, and the blues.

At first, R&B was called "race music," a way of referring to almost any music made by black musicians for black audiences. But by the time World War II ended, that term was considered offensive.

In the late 1940s, a writer for *Billboard* magazine began calling it "rhythm and blues" in an effort to capture the high-energy, more rock and roll–like sound that all kinds of fans—both black and white—were listening to.

Early R&B legend Fats Domino

But for the sheer joy of it, Stevie kept right on singing in his neighborhood—on street corners and on front porches. People gathered to hear Stevie play the harmonica and sing with his friend John Glover.

John, who was three years older than Stevie, played the guitar. He was the son of one of Lula's friends. He had a cousin named Ronnie White, who was a member of the singing group the Miracles.

In 1961, John Glover asked Ronnie White to listen to Stevie sing. As a favor to his cousin, Ronnie agreed. He didn't expect to be amazed. "But I knew he would be," John said. "Everybody who saw Stevie always was."

Sure enough, Ronnie could barely believe the power of Stevie's talent. Ronnie told Stevie that he would take him to see the president of Motown Records the very next day.

The Miracles

The Miracles were the first big stars of Motown Records.

Their lead singer and songwriter, Smokey Robinson, formed the group with Ronald White and Warren "Pete" Moore. The Miracles had been a popular rhythm-and-blues singing group in the Detroit area. They decided to join Berry Gordy Jr. when he founded Motown Records in 1959.

The Miracles became famous in 1960, when their hit record "Shop Around" sold more than one million copies. They went on to record thirty-eight Top 40 hits, including "The Tracks of My Tears" and "The Tears of a Clown."

The Miracles were inducted into the Rock and Roll Hall of Fame in 2012.

CHAPTER 3
Little Stevie

Stevie walked into Motown Records on a September day in 1961 with his mother, John Glover, and Ronnie White. The sign above the door said "Hitsville, U.S.A." The truth was that

Motown didn't have very many hits (top-selling records) yet. It was a young company trying to grow. When the man who had founded Motown, Berry Gordy, heard Stevie audition, he believed Stevie could help Motown grow.

The energy Stevie had, the feeling he brought to his songs, and the way people responded to him all convinced Mr. Gordy that Stevie could be a star.

Berry Gordy Jr.

Motown Record Corporation

Berry Gordy opened the Motown recording studio in his hometown of Detroit in 1959. Motown's name is a shortened version of the nickname for Detroit: "Motor City," or "Motor Town." It was called that because for many decades almost all American cars were made there.

Motown is important in the history of American music because it brought its unique sound to both black and white audiences at a time before any other company had bridged that gap. That new sound was a version of rhythm and blues that included elements of blues, gospel, jazz, country, and pop music. Motown produced seventy-nine top-ten records during the 1960s, when it became one of the most successful black-owned businesses in the United States.

In 1972 the company left Detroit and relocated to the Capitol Records building in Los Angeles.

Mr. Gordy didn't really like to sign performers who were under eighteen years old because there were strict laws about the hours they could work, the number of days they could be away from home on tour, and the amount of time they must spend on their schooling. But he knew Stevie's talent was worth making an exception. He decided that very day in the studio he wanted to offer Stevie a contract with Motown Records.

It took a few days to work out the details, but Stevie returned to Motown with Lula to sign his contract. He was officially a professional musician!

Soon Stevie was rushing over to the recording studio at Motown every day after school. He spent most of his time there—more time than he did at home. Lula did not mind. She saw that the people at Motown took good care of Stevie. Clarence Paul worked with Stevie as his producer, and he was like a father to him. Ted Hull was hired as a tutor to make sure Stevie didn't fall behind in his studies.

Stevie would listen to B. B. King and other current stars on his small, portable transistor radio on the bus on his way over to the studio, then get to hear other Motown talent, such as the Temptations, the Supremes, Mary Wells, and Marvin Gaye, performing live in the studio.

Mr. Gordy liked to call his Motown performers a family. And, if Motown was a family, Stevie was their fun—and sometimes annoying—little brother. He enjoyed hanging around the other musicians, interrupting their recording sessions, and playing pranks.

Stevie could imitate Berry Gordy's voice perfectly—so well that not even his secretary could tell the difference. Once, when the Motown boss was away on business, Stevie called Mr. Gordy's secretary and asked her to give Stevie a tape recorder when he came into the studio. That day, Stevie arrived and was handed the tape recorder.

Because he was blind, Stevie couldn't see the red light that warned when a recording session was in progress. Sometimes, he accidentally walked in and ruined sessions for the other musicians.

But no one could stay mad at Stevie very long. He was so happy to be playing music at Motown that he was like a kid in a candy store—only his candy store was a recording studio!

"Hey, how do you do this?" Stevie would ask the other performers. "How do you do that?" He wanted to learn everything he could about becoming a better musician. Stevie was enthusiastic and almost always had a smile on his face.

And he was talented, too. More than once, someone at Motown remarked that little Stevie was a wonder. "And the nickname just stuck," said Mr. Gordy. The Motown boss began promoting his new star as Little Stevie Wonder.

CHAPTER 4
Fingertips

Everyone at Motown agreed that Little Stevie was a real wonder, but now what? He was only eleven years old. Would he sing love songs? Or play high-energy dance tunes? Or show off his talent at playing the harmonica and other instruments? No one could quite figure out exactly where he fit into the musical picture.

Stevie's first album, *The Jazz Soul of Little Stevie*, was released in September 1962. It was an instrumental. That meant that there were no words to any of the songs. Stevie played the bongos, keyboard, harmonica, and other instruments on the album, but he didn't sing at all. Unfortunately, the album didn't sell very well.

Just one month later, Stevie's second album was released: *Tribute to Uncle Ray*. "Uncle Ray" was Ray Charles, a famous singer who was not actually related to Stevie, but who was also blind. Ray Charles was twenty years older than Stevie.

On his tribute album, Stevie sang Ray's popular songs. But this second album didn't sell very well, either.

Sadly, Stevie's early recordings didn't capture the fun and excitement he showed when he played for friends or studio executives. Whenever there was an audience present, Stevie seemed to really come alive. So Berry Gordy sent Stevie on a tour called the Motortown Revue late in 1962.

Stevie joined Marvin Gaye, the Miracles, the Supremes, the Temptations, and other acts on the Motortown Revue. They rode two old buses and several cars into thirty-six cities over fifty-six days. They performed almost every night.

It was an exhausting tour, especially for twelve-year-old Stevie.

Ray Charles (1930–2004)

Ray Charles Robinson was a singer, songwriter, and pianist who is sometimes called the "The Genius" for the way he combined different forms of music—including gospel, R&B, and jazz—to create the style we now call "soul." He is also known as the "Father of Soul Music."

Charles grew up in poverty in the South. He lost his sight due to an illness at age seven. He developed a talent for music at the Florida School for the Deaf and the Blind, and he was still a teenager when he began performing professionally.

His most famous hits all came in the early 1960s and included "Unchain My Heart," "Hit the Road Jack," and "Georgia on My Mind." In 1986, Ray Charles was among the first group of inductees to the Rock and Roll Hall of Fame.

Until the tour, Stevie had little experience with racism. Kids had called him names before, but he had never felt racial intolerance like he did while on the tour. Some of the stops were at mostly white towns in the South, where racism was still strong. In some cities, Stevie was not allowed to eat in the same restaurants or use the same bathrooms that white people did. After one show in Birmingham, Alabama, the performers heard gunshots as they were leaving. Later, the driver found bullet holes in the "Motortown Revue" sign on one of their buses.

Near the end of the tour, the group was happy to arrive in more tolerant cities such as New York, where they performed at the Apollo Theater in Harlem.

Little Stevie was a big hit with the audiences on tour. He sometimes stayed on the stage playing far longer than he was supposed to. Clarence Paul occasionally had to come onstage and drag Stevie off!

The Apollo Theater

The Apollo Theater is a famous music hall in the Harlem neighborhood of New York City. When it opened in 1914 as the Hurtig and Seamon's New Burlesque Theater, it had a "whites only" policy. Blacks could not perform or watch shows there.

In 1934, it became the Apollo Theater. It opened its doors to black performers and audiences, and it went on to become the place "where stars are born and legends are made." Monday evening was "amateur night in Harlem," where talented unknown performers were invited to take the stage and win over audiences.

The Apollo, which is still open today, has helped launch the careers of many superstars, including Stevie Wonder, the Jackson 5, James Brown, Lauryn Hill, and Mariah Carey.

APOLLO
AMATEUR NIGHT
AT THE APOLLO

Because he often invited the audience to sing and clap along with him, some famous performers found it difficult to go on after Stevie. After one performance, Diana Ross, the lead singer of the Supremes, asked, "How are we supposed to follow that?"

At the Regal Theater in Chicago in early 1963, Stevie began playing the bongos when he walked onstage and, as usual, had the crowd involved right away. "I want you to clap your hands," he told the audience. "Come on! Come on! Yeah! Stomp your feet, jump up and down, do anything that you want to do! Yeah! Yeah!"

Stevie was about to play the song called "Fingertips," which had been on his first album. However, instead of playing "Fingertips" on the bongos like he usually did, Stevie grabbed his harmonica and played it on that. When the song was over, with the crowd on its feet, Paul escorted Stevie off the stage.

But Stevie returned and continued to play. The surprised band members tried to keep up as Stevie launched into another lively version of the song. The crowd went wild!

Several months later, Mr. Gordy had an unusual idea. He'd release Stevie's live Chicago performance. It was unusual to release a live performance as a seven-inch single record.

On that single, the public was able to hear the *real* Stevie in action. The joy of his music came through, and fans loved it.

One side of the record was "Fingertips." The other side was "Fingertips, Part 2"—the second part of the song Stevie had played after returning to the stage at the Regal Theater. "Fingertips, Part 2" soared up the record charts.

Everybody—black audiences and white audiences—seemed to love "Fingertips, Part 2." The record sold more than one million copies and was number one on both *Billboard*'s Hot 100 and R&B (rhythm and blues) lists. No other song had ever been number one on the two charts at the same time before.

The *Billboard* Charts

When Stevie Wonder began his career in the early 1960s, people listened to music on the radio or by playing vinyl (plastic) records on turntables.

In 1940, *Billboard* magazine began tracking the popularity of songs based on record sales and how often they were played on the radio. They published their rankings each week on the *Billboard* charts.

Billboard continues to rank music singles in the *Billboard* Hot 100 and albums in the *Billboard* 200. The magazine publishes rankings in many different categories such as country, rock, latin, jazz, dance/electronic, R&B/hip-hop.

The single was included on Stevie's first successful album: *Recorded Live: The 12-Year-Old Genius*. Stevie was thirteen by the time the album was finished and sold in stores. It became the first Motown album to reach number one on the *Billboard* charts.

"Fingertips, Part 2" was a huge hit. Marvin Gaye, who had played drums on the song, said, "You really had to start paying attention to Stevie after 'Fingertips.'"

CHAPTER 5
Not So Little Anymore

Because "Fingertips, Part 2" was so successful, everyone wanted to have the chance to see Stevie. He appeared on national television programs such as *The Ed Sullivan Show*. He performed in London and Paris. When the Motortown Revue went on the road again late in 1963, he was billed as one of its top stars. He even appeared in two "beach party" movies—silly teen comedies with lots of singing and dancing.

But Little Stevie wasn't so little anymore. He was five feet nine inches tall by the time he was fourteen years old. And he was becoming a big star. Motown dropped "Little" from his name. Stevie Wonder was ready to follow up his first big hit.

Most of Stevie's early songs had been written by other people and were simple tunes with simple lyrics. Stevie started getting frustrated. "Why don't they just let me sing my own songs?" he complained to a fellow Motown performer. "I'd be doing a lot better if I can sing what I want to sing."

So he sat down with Motown songwriters Hank Cosby and Sylvia Moy and wrote a song about a poor boy dating a rich girl. "Uptight (Everything's Alright)" was released in November 1965 and spent five weeks at number one on the R&B chart.

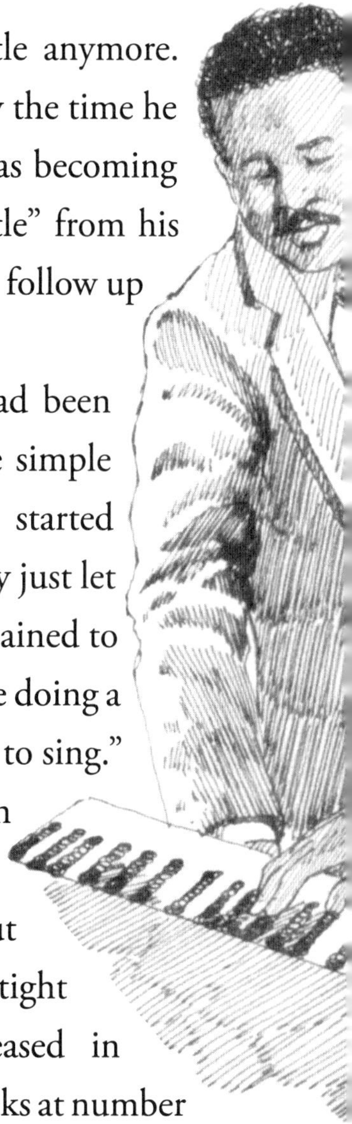

More hits followed over the next couple of years, including "Shoo-Be-Doo-Be-Doo-Da-Day," "For Once in My Life," "My Cherie Amour," and "Yester-Me, Yester-You, Yesterday." Stevie already had recorded ten albums and had seven top-ten singles by the time he graduated from the Michigan School for the Blind with a high-school diploma in June 1969. He was just nineteen years old.

Around that time, one of Stevie's favorite songs was "I Can't Give Back the Love I Feel for You," by Syreeta (Rita) Wright. Stevie wanted to meet Syreeta,

Syreeta Wright

who also worked for Motown. After he did, the two began working together on a song: "You Win My Love." The song was never released but, Syreeta said, Stevie won her love. In 1970, when Stevie was twenty years old, he and Syreeta were married. Unfortunately, the marriage lasted less than two years.

Syreeta had helped Stevie write the single "Signed, Sealed, Delivered I'm Yours," which reached number three on the *Billboard* Hot 100 and number one on the R&B chart. Stevie's mom also earned a writing credit on that song because she came up with the line used in the chorus and the title.

One day Stevie was at home working on lyrics, singing, "Here I am, baby. Here I am, baby." Lula sang out, "Signed, sealed, delivered, I'm yours."

"Signed, Sealed, Delivered I'm Yours" was a smash hit. By that time, Stevie had been writing many songs—sometimes dozens at a time. Some were only a few lines, and some weren't much more than ideas. But he had so much music inside of him that he kept a tape recorder with him most of the time so he wouldn't forget anything that came into his mind.

The trouble was, many of Stevie's new songs were not the kind Motown was interested in. Motown wanted positive lyrics and catchy tunes with a beat that listeners could dance to. Stevie knew that, but he wanted to sing about the more realistic side of life. "Just because a man lacks the use of his eyes doesn't mean he lacks vision," he once said.

Berry Gordy had a system in place at Motown—a system he felt would ensure that the acts that worked for the label would become successful. He gave his performers classes on manners, grooming, and how to dress for the part. In exchange, most of the money from their record sales went to Mr. Gordy. Stevie recognized that the Motown system worked in the beginning of his career because he received so much help from Mr. Gordy. But now he felt ready to take more control of his career.

Stevie knew that his contract expired once he turned twenty-one years old in 1971. He could choose to stay with Motown, sign with another record company, or work on his own. He decided to work on his own.

Using his money, he began making an album called *Music of My Mind* that had a unique sound. Stevie had discovered the synthesizer.

In the recording studio, a synthesizer had been simply a way of saving money. It could take the place of both the musician and the instrument. But for Stevie, the synthesizer was a way of re-creating sounds that he could not achieve with any other instrument.

The Synthesizer

The synthesizer is an instrument that can create music from electronic signals and is often played with a keyboard. It can be used to imitate other instruments, depending on the way the signal is controlled.

Although by the 1970s some form of the synthesizer had been around for nearly one hundred years, it was still relatively new to recorded music, in part because it was very large and difficult to operate.

But Stevie worked out a deal with Berry Gordy so *Music of My Mind* could be distributed and sold by Motown beginning in March 1972. The album sounded nothing like anything that had ever been released by Motown. The songs were longer than most Motown pop tunes, and Stevie played all the instruments on all the songs himself except for the trombone and guitar.

When *Music of My Mind* reached number six on the R&B chart, Mr. Gordy knew he couldn't let Stevie leave Motown for another record company.

Stevie eventually signed a new five-year contract with Motown, but for terms that no other musician with the company had ever been granted: a massive $1 million, plus the freedom to make any music that he wanted.

CHAPTER 6
Superstar

Ever since he was a teenager, Stevie's music had been popular with a broad audience, both black and white. With *Music of My Mind*, Stevie's fan base grew even larger. In 1972, he went on tour with the Rolling Stones, one of the most popular rock-and-roll bands in the world.

Stevie was the opening act, the performer who plays before the main attraction. But it wasn't long before Mick Jagger, the lead singer of the Rolling Stones, was bringing Stevie back onstage to join him in singing "Satisfaction,"

one of the group's biggest hits. The crowd loved Stevie—maybe a little too much. Some of the tour's organizers thought he was taking too much attention from the Stones. But Mick insisted that Stevie stay. Onstage, they were a good mix.

Offstage, they were very different. The Rolling Stones often had parties filled with drinking and illegal drugs. Stevie did not do those things.

Illegal drug use, as well as violence and crime, were on the rise in the seventies—especially in big cities in the United States.

Stevie felt those were important issues that needed to be addressed, and he wanted his music to be a part of that conversation. He began writing more about the reality of racism and poverty. His next album, *Talking Book*, showed the world that an R&B artist could appeal to audiences that usually listened to rock music.

Talking Book's "You Are the Sunshine of My Life" was a love song that soared to number one on the charts and earned Stevie a Grammy award—the awards given each year by the National Academy of Recording Arts and Sciences for outstanding performances in music. "Superstition," a funky, high-energy song, went to number one, too, and won two Grammys.

Talking Book included a message from Stevie to his fans written in braille on the cardboard cover. "Here is my music," it read. "It is all I have to tell you how I feel. Know that your love keeps my love strong." The album was a huge hit for Stevie.

Just a year later, Stevie released an album called *Innervisions*. Its most memorable song was "Living for the City," about a black man from the South who moves to New York City and is arrested and sentenced to ten years in jail. The song used noise from the street—traffic and sirens and voices—to bring the sounds of the city directly into the story. "Living for the City" was a number one hit on the R&B chart. So was "Higher Ground," another song from the album.

In August 1973, just three days after *Innervisions* was released, Stevie was involved in a terrible car accident. On his way to a concert in North Carolina, a log fell off a truck and crashed through the windshield of the car in which Stevie was riding. It struck Stevie in the face. Stevie spent several days in a coma and nearly died. No one was sure if he would be able to sing, write, or play music again.

Braille

Braille is a system of reading and writing used by the blind. It uses a series of raised dots that represent letters, numbers, and punctuation marks. The dots are read by touch.

Braille is named after Louis Braille.

At age three, he was blinded by an accident in his father's workshop. In 1824, when he was just fifteen, Louis first developed the system that is now used by people around the world who cannot see or have difficulty seeing.

But the accident didn't lessen Stevie's passion for music or his positive outlook on life. "Anyone who has had such an event never looks at life quite the same way," he said. "I felt it was a second chance at life."

He wasn't about to let that chance go to waste.

Only one month after the accident, Stevie made a brief appearance at an Elton John concert. And in March 1974, he returned to the stage for an emotional concert at Madison Square Garden in New York City.

Stevie's already successful career reached its own "higher ground" in the months that followed. *Innervisions* won the Grammy for Album of the Year in 1973. Then his next album, *Fulfillingness' First Finale*, won Album of the Year in 1974. Amazingly, Stevie won Album of the Year again in 1976 with *Songs in the Key of Life*, which is the signature album of his career.

Songs in the Key of Life is considered to be among the best albums of all time. It is preserved in the Library of Congress's National Recording Registry for its historical significance.

On the album, Stevie continued to address issues of racism and poverty with songs such as "Black Man" and "Village Ghetto Land." But he also wrote about people who inspired him. "Sir Duke" is a tribute to the jazz legend Duke Ellington.

Duke Ellington (1899–1974)

Edward Kennedy "Duke" Ellington was an internationally famous pianist, songwriter, and bandleader who led the Duke Ellington Orchestra for more than fifty years. Though often considered a jazz legend, Ellington preferred to call his music "American music." He composed more than a thousand songs in his lifetime. Among his band's lasting hits were "It Don't Mean a Thing (If It Ain't Got That Swing)" and "Take the 'A' Train."

Stevie recorded most of *Songs in the Key of Life* in Hollywood. When he wasn't on the road performing, he spent most of his time there. He wanted his mother closer to him, so he bought Lula a large home nearby. He also had a daughter with his girlfriend, Yolanda Simmons. "Isn't She Lovely," one of the most popular songs from *Songs in the Key of Life*, was Stevie's tribute to his baby girl, Aisha.

When Stevie's contract with Motown ended in the late 1970s, he broke music industry records by re-signing with the label for a guaranteed $13 million, to be paid over seven years. His first two albums under the new contract made the expense worth it for Mr. Gordy. *Stevie Wonder's Journey Through "The Secret Life of Plants"* reached number four on the R&B charts. *Hotter Than July* was number one.

CHAPTER 7
Making a Difference

Stevie's music reflected the things that were important to him. But in the 1980s he began taking a more active role in those causes. He played concerts to support peace rallies. He protested against the South African system of racial segregation known as apartheid.

Stevie even made goodwill visits to foreign countries to help raise money for many different charities.

Stevie felt especially strongly about one particular issue: that Dr. Martin Luther King Jr.'s birthday should become a national holiday. Many other people did, too. But several tries at creating the new holiday had failed.

Dr. Martin Luther King Jr.

The cause was so important to Stevie that in the early 1980s, he put much of his music career on hold and spent his time trying to convince politicians to support the holiday. In 1981, he released a single called "Happy Birthday." In "Happy Birthday," Stevie sang:

I just never understood
How a man who died for good
Could not have a day that would
Be set aside for his recognition

Stevie wondered how anyone could oppose creating a national Martin Luther King Jr. Day.

Stevie gave performances and made speeches to support the national holiday. In 1981, he hosted a Rally for Peace Press Conference with civil rights leaders such as Reverend Jesse Jackson. In 1982, he led a rally in Washington on Dr. King's birthday that featured other stars such as singers Gladys Knight and Diana Ross. More than fifty thousand people attended. "Why should I be involved in this great

cause?" Stevie asked the crowd. "As an artist, my purpose is to communicate the message that can better improve the lives of *all* of us."

Stevie could have made much more money playing concerts and releasing new songs. But for Stevie, it was worth it to spend his time working on a day to honor Dr. King. His four years of hard work paid off when Congress passed a bill creating the holiday. President Ronald Reagan signed it into law on November 2, 1983. Now, with Dr. King's birthday officially a national holiday, Stevie went back to work on his music.

Martin Luther King Jr. (1929–1968)

The Reverend Dr. Martin Luther King Jr. was one of the leaders of the civil rights movement in the United States in the 1960s. The movement sought to gain equal rights for black people in America. At the time, black people could still legally be treated different from whites—for instance, by being forced to eat

in different restaurants or stay in different hotels.

Dr. King tried to change that by organizing peaceful rallies and demonstrations.

In 1963, Dr. King gave his famous "I Have a Dream" speech while standing in front of the Lincoln Memorial in Washington, DC, during the March on Washington for Jobs and Freedom.

Dr. King was assassinated in Memphis, Tennessee, in 1968.

In 1984, Stevie wrote and recorded the soundtrack for a movie called *The Woman in Red.* It was not a great movie, the critics generally agreed, but it had an excellent soundtrack. The following spring, a single from the album, "I Just Called to Say I Love You" earned Stevie an Academy Award for Best Original Song. (The Academy Awards are the movie industry's annual top honors.) When Stevie accepted his award, he dedicated it to Nelson Mandela, a civil rights leader who was imprisoned in his native country, South Africa.

In May 1985, Stevie was honored by the United Nations for speaking out against apartheid in South Africa. That same year, Stevie joined some of the biggest names in the music industry for a benefit song called "We Are the World." Profits from the sales of the song were sent to help fight hunger and disease throughout the continent of Africa.

USA for Africa

A supergroup of forty-four musicians called USA for Africa came together in Hollywood, California, to record "We Are the World." The song was written by megastars Michael Jackson and Lionel Richie. It sold more than twenty million copies and helped raise more than $63 million.

Some of the famous people who were a part of the USA for Africa group were Ray Charles, Billy Joel, Diana Ross, Bruce Springsteen, Dionne Warwick, Bob Dylan, Tina Turner, and Willie Nelson.

In 1989, Stevie was inducted into the Rock and Roll Hall of Fame. He was only thirty-eight years old at the time. He had won fourteen Grammy awards and an Academy Award. He helped create a national holiday. He worked to raise awareness about racism and hunger around the world. What was next for Stevie Wonder?

CHAPTER 8
Living Legend

In 2009, Stevie was named a United Nations Messenger of Peace. "He has consistently used his voice and special relationship with the public to create a better and more inclusive world, to defend civil and human rights, and to improve the lives of those less fortunate," said UN Secretary-General Ban Ki-moon. "Stevie Wonder is a true inspiration to young people all over the world about what can be achieved despite any physical limitations."

By then, Stevie was a friend to several world leaders. In the early 1990s, the president of Ghana invited Stevie to visit the West African country. In his six weeks there in 1993, Stevie wrote many of the songs that appeared on his album *Conversation Peace*.

Stevie rejoiced at the end of apartheid in South Africa in 1994 and, two years later, met Nelson Mandela, who had been elected the president of South Africa. In 1998, he performed for President Bill Clinton and British Prime Minister Tony Blair at the White House.

Nelson Mandela (1918–2013)

Nelson Mandela was outspoken against apartheid, the official policy of racial segregation (separation) in South Africa that lasted from 1948 to 1994. For organizing against the unfairness of apartheid, Mandela spent twenty-seven years in jail. After his release in 1990, he helped negotiate with the South African government for the end of apartheid. Mandela then was elected president of South Africa, a position he held until 1999.

Stevie married again in 2001. His wife, Kai Millard, was a fashion designer. That marriage lasted eleven years. Stevie and Kai had two children together.

In 2004 Stevie's brother Larry died of cancer. Two years later, Lula died at age seventy-six. Stevie was saddened, but kept on performing. "I want to take all the pain that I feel and celebrate and turn it around," he said after Lula died.

Stevie continued to perform and was on the road again in 2014 and 2015 with his Songs in the Key of Life Tour. November 2016 was the

fortieth anniversary of Stevie's most popular album. Many famous musicians, including Prince and Elton John, have stated that *Songs in the Key of Life* is one of the greatest albums ever made.

"Stevie has a unique voice, and a unique soul that feeds that voice," Motown founder Berry Gordy once said. "Whenever he sings any song, it brings up the love, the soul, the feeling."

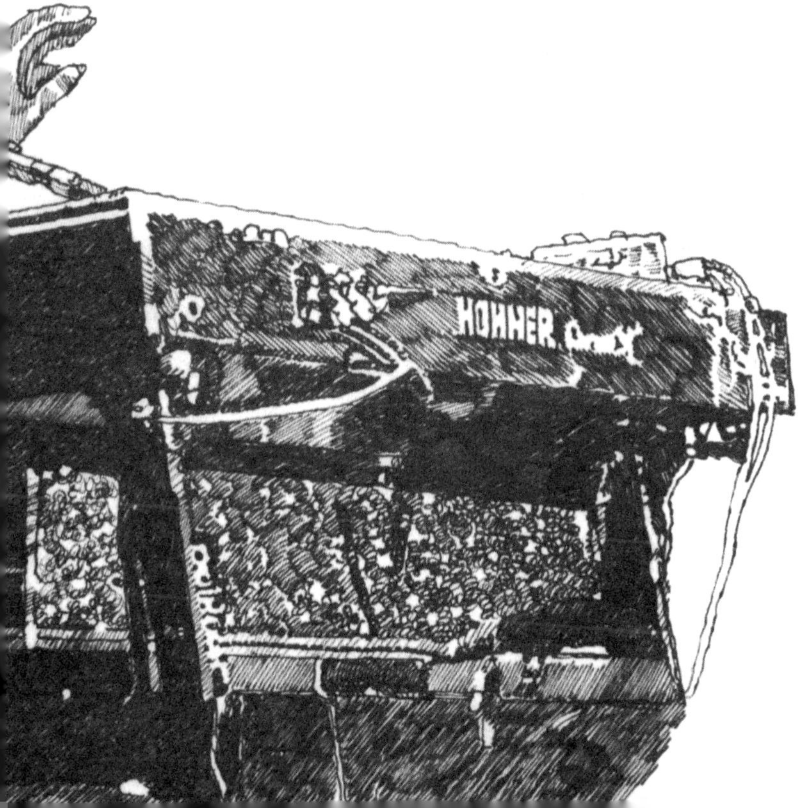

In November 2014, at a ceremony at the White House in Washington, DC, President Barack Obama presented Stevie with the Presidential Medal of Freedom. It's the highest civilian award in the United States.

President Obama called Stevie's work "the soundtrack to my youth." He went on to say, "For more than fifty years, Stevie has channeled his inner visions into messages of hope and healing, becoming one of the most influential musicians in American history."

Stevie's songs have influenced a huge variety of artists across all musical styles. He has entertained a wide range of audiences, too. Young or old, rich or poor, black or white—everyone seems to have a favorite Stevie Wonder song.

And Stevie has accomplished everything he has despite never having the gift of sight. He has always kept his smile, joy, and sense of humor. "Do you know, it's funny, but I never thought of being blind as a disadvantage," he says.

Stevie is an inspiration to many. He is a recording legend. He is a champion of equality and justice. But, as he likes to say, if you *really* want to know who Stevie Wonder is, just listen to his music.

Timeline of Stevie Wonder's Life

1950	Stevie Wonder is born Steveland Hardaway Judkins on May 13 in Saginaw, Michigan
1961	Auditions at the Motown recording studio and is signed to a contract by Motown founder Berry Gordy
1962	Releases first single, "I Call It Pretty Music," under the name Little Stevie Wonder
1963	"Fingertips, Part 2" reaches number one on *Billboard* magazine's Hot 100
1969	Earns his high-school diploma at the Michigan School for the Blind
1971	Turns twenty-one and eventually signs a new contract with Motown that gives him significant control over his work
1972	Tours with the Rolling Stones
1974	Wins the first four of his twenty-five career Grammy awards, with *Innervisions* awarded Album of the Year
1975	Daughter Aisha, the inspiration for Stevie's "Isn't She Lovely," is born
1985	Wins the Academy Award for Best Original Song ("I Just Called to Say I Love You" from *The Woman in Red*)
1989	Inducted into the Rock and Roll Hall of Fame
2004	Receives the Century Achievement Award, the "highest honor for creative achievement," from *Billboard* magazine
2014	Presented with the Presidential Medal of Freedom in a ceremony at the White House

Timeline of the World

1947	Jackie Robinson of the Brooklyn Dodgers becomes the first black player in the modern era of Major League Baseball
1951	Color television is introduced to the public
1954	The United States Supreme Court rules that racial segregation in schools is unconstitutional
1959	The first annual Grammy awards are held to recognize outstanding achievement in the music industry
1963	John F. Kennedy, the president of the United States, is assassinated
1964	Beatlemania sweeps across the United States
1968	Civil rights leader Dr. Martin Luther King Jr. is assassinated
1969	American Neil Armstrong becomes the first man to walk on the moon
1974	Richard Nixon resigns as president of the United States after the Watergate scandal
1976	Steve Jobs and Steve Wozniak start Apple Computer, Inc.
1981	New cable television channel MTV launches with music videos aimed at younger audiences
1986	Dr. Martin Luther King Jr.'s birth date, January 15, is celebrated as a national holiday in the United States for the first time
1997	The first Harry Potter novel is published in the United Kingdom
2008	Barack Obama is elected the first black president of the United States

Bibliography

*** Books for young readers**

* Brown, Jeremy K. ***Stevie Wonder: Musician.*** Philadelphia: Chelsea House Publishers, 2010.

Lodder, Steve. ***Stevie Wonder: A Musical Guide to the Classic Albums.*** San Francisco: Backbeat Books, 2005.

Love, Dennis, and Stacy Brown. ***Blind Faith: The Miraculous Journey of Lula Hardaway, Stevie Wonder's Mother***. New York: Simon & Schuster, 2002.

Perone, James E. ***The Sound of Stevie Wonder: His Words and Music***. Westport, CT: Praeger Publishers, 2006.

Ribowsky, Mark. ***Signed, Sealed, and Delivered: The Soulful Journey of Stevie Wonder***. Hoboken, NJ: John Wiley & Sons, 2010.

* Troupe, Quincy. ***Little Stevie Wonder***. Boston: Houghton Mifflin Company, 2005.

* Williams, Tenley. ***Stevie Wonder***. Overcoming Adversity. Philadelphia: Chelsea House Publishers, 2002.